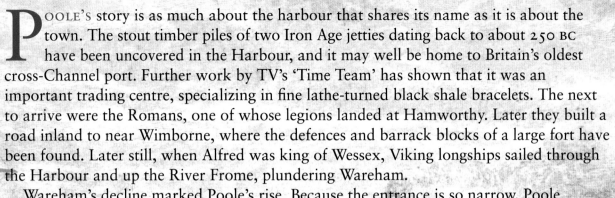

POOLE'S story is as much about the harbour that shares its name as it is about the town. The stout timber piles of two Iron Age jetties dating back to about 250 BC have been uncovered in the Harbour, and it may well be home to Britain's oldest cross-Channel port. Further work by TV's 'Time Team' has shown that it was an important trading centre, specializing in fine lathe-turned black shale bracelets. The next to arrive were the Romans, one of whose legions landed at Hamworthy. Later they built a road inland to near Wimborne, where the defences and barrack blocks of a large fort have been found. Later still, when Alfred was king of Wessex, Viking longships sailed through the Harbour and up the River Frome, plundering Wareham.

Wareham's decline marked Poole's rise. Because the entrance is so narrow, Poole Harbour is blessed with a double high tide. But the tides are strong, and boats making the long passage to Wareham risked running aground as their draughts grew deeper and the channel began silting up. The tiny fishing village of 'La Pole' was closer to the open sea, its channel deeper. Despite the impact of the

*Above* Poole's medieval and Georgian past face each other in Church Street, with the Guildhall visible in the distance. The warm brick and classical doorways are typical of the old town. On the right are St George's Almshouses, originally built by the Guild of St George in about 1429, when Henry V was king. The Guild combined praying for the souls of its deceased members with taking care of those in need. Much altered and modernized, the Almshouses continue to provide accommodation for the elderly in the heart of the town.

# The Old Town

Black Death and occasional raids by the French, Poole prospered and by the late middle ages it was Dorset's largest port, infamous for its pirates. Bales of cloth and wool packed the Town Cellars ready for shipping abroad. Returning vessels landed wine and salt on the Great Quay. On the landward side it was protected by a tidal dyke, and its bustling streets of tightly packed houses could only be entered through a massive stone gateway.

Poole's golden age was the eighteenth century, and it was founded almost entirely on one product – cod. The discovery of enormous shoals of cod off the Newfoundland coast led to what became known as the triangular trade. Every spring the Poole fishing fleet of up to 300 vessels weighed anchor and headed west across the Atlantic to the fishing grounds,

their holds laden with goods and supplies for the settlers. The catch was dried and salted. Together with barrels of cod oil, it was then either shipped to the Caribbean for the slaves on the plantations, or – more commonly – to Catholic Europe (Spain, Portugal, Italy), from where the fleet returned to Poole with either Caribbean rum and sugar or Mediterranean wine, olive oil and dried fruit. Poole grew wealthy, attracting the tradesmen and craftsmen needed to equip the fleet. The town's surviving mansions were paid for by the fortunes made by its merchants.

The boom years could not last. Once peace had returned to Europe after Napoleon's defeat at Waterloo in 1815 the Newfoundland trade collapsed. The arrival of the railway meant fewer ships docking alongside the Quay. Elegant Georgian townhouses became tenements. Even oysters, the one surviving harvest from the sea, died out from over-dredging. Ironically, the town was saved from further decline by its

*Above left* The Mansion House in Thames Street, where two fillets of dried cod carved in marble above a fireplace celebrate the source of the fortune that paid for it. The house, now an hotel, was started by Isaac Lester in 1776, and completed by his brother Benjamin, later Poole's MP and one of the great figures of Georgian Poole. By the 1780s his 30 vessel shipping fleet was catching 400,000 cod a year off Newfoundland. His daughter married into another of Poole's merchant prince families, the Garlands, who had forged close links with the growing coastal settlements in Newfoundland.

*Left* Stone urns and pineapples line the baroque façade of West End House, on the corner of Thames Street and St James's Close. It was built by the Newfoundland merchant John Slade in about 1740 and was later the home of Jesse Carter, an ironmonger who transformed a small pottery on the Quay making Victorian floor tiles into what became the renowned Poole Pottery.

*Above* The Guildhall was built in 1761 and largely paid for by Poole's two MPs, who each contributed £750. The ground floor is now enclosed, but originally was open at one end and used as a market, whilst the upper floor housed the Corporation offices and council chamber. Since then it has also served as a magistrates court, the Court of Admiralty, a temporary parish church, a wartime canteen for American servicemen, a classroom for Poole College, and as Poole's museum. Today it houses the town's Registration Services for births, deaths and marriages and is much used for weddings.

*Above left* One of the tragedies of modern Poole is the wholesale demolition of much of its architectural heritage in the late 1950s and early 1960s. Until then much of old Poole was a warren of alleys, passageways and narrow streets lined with fine Georgian townhouses. This view is of St James's Close.

*Left* Poole's coat of arms, with its mermaid, dolphin and scallop shells. The shells are the badge of St James, to whom Poole's parish church is dedicated. The Latin translates as 'According to the Custom of the Town of Poole' and comes from the Charter of 1568 granted by Elizabeth I, which established it as a county in its own right and recognized the port's growing importance by exempting its merchants from all import duties. This particular coat-of-arms in stained glass came from Corfe Mullen Waterworks and is now in Poole Museum.

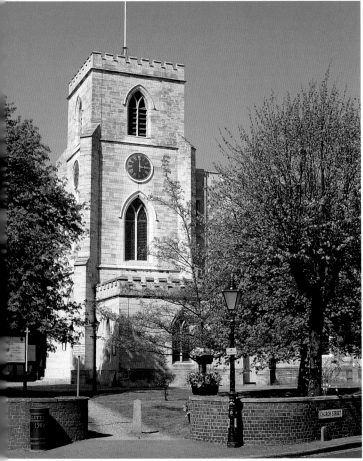

St James's Church. Although some of the stone and wall memorials were retained, the original parish church was knocked down in 1819 and replaced by the present church, whose stout tower can still be seen above the surrounding rooftops when landing at the Quay by boat. The church sits at the heart of the tiny fragment of Georgian Poole to survive, and as well as the nautical nets and flags it contains several reminders of the Newfoundland trade, most prominently the wooden columns cut from Newfoundland pine.

youthful upstart neighbour, Bournemouth. Bournemouth's dramatic growth from hamlet to prosperous resort gave new life to Poole. Brick and pottery works opened. Coasters returned to the Quay with grain, coal and iron. The great Baltic sailing ships brought timber and tar. By the dawn of the twentieth century Poole was expanding inland over the heath and out towards the still desolate Sandbanks peninsula. In Hamworthy, Lake, Upton, Parkstone, Canford Cliffs and Lilliput, newly laid-out streets filled with terraces of shops and trim brick-built villas.

# The Quay

The Harbour Office and the Quay

By the outbreak of the Second World War Poole Harbour was Britain's principal flying boat base. The war brought barbed wire to the beaches. Brownsea Island became temporary home to Dutch refugees fleeing Occupied Holland. A Special Services base of Commandos and Royal Marines was established at Hamworthy. As D-Day approached, the Quay was taken over by the Americans and their landing craft and armed high-speed cutters.

Over the last 60 years Poole has grown immeasurably. One casualty has been the heathland, whose irreplaceable flora and fauna is constantly under threat by the need for housing

and industrial development. On the credit side, Poole's trading estates, manufacturing base and offices have provided employment, and a new sense of optimism and prosperity. Happily, the town's reputation and the presence of the sea have made it as attractive to the young as it is to the retired. Few summer visitors leave without enjoying a boat trip, a visit to Brownsea Island or a lazy day on the beaches. But the traditional heart of the town, as it has been for 1000 years, is the Quay – always busy with boats, the perfect promenade for a morning stroll, and against whose ancient walls lap the waters of what is surely the most beautiful natural harbour in Britain.

*Above* Fishing boats alongside the Quay. Behind it are (from left to right) the Harbour Office, Town Cellars and Custom House.

*Below* The Fisherman's Dock is home to the small locally-registered fishing boats that help give the Harbour its character. In the foreground is a memorial stone commemmorating an American Coast Guard Rescue Flotilla based at Poole during the Normany landings of 1944, during which they rescued 1437 men and one woman.

*Above* Matching flights of stone steps curve up to the entrance of the elegant Custom House on the Quay, now a restaurant and café. It was built in 1813, replacing an earlier building, when Poole's golden age still had a few years to run and the Quay was crowded with vessels landing skins, wine, spices and oil. From here, carts laden with fish trundled inland to the markets in Dorset's towns, whilst Purbeck stone and locally dug clay went by ship to London. The pillars belong to the Georgian Harbour Office, whilst beyond on the left are what were the 15th century Town Cellars, where wool from flocks grazing the nearby downland was once stored. It was originally much longer, but still remains one of the best examples of a medieval woolhouse in Britain.

*Right* Pleasure boats tout their rival cruises alongside the Quay in summer. There's something for everyone, from trips up the River Frome to Wareham, days spent fishing in Poole Bay, tours of Poole Harbour, or cruises to either Bournemouth or Swanage.

*Above*  Crabbing from the Quay at Fisherman's Dock can keep 'children' of all ages happy for hours. The brick building was once Poole Lifeboat Station and is now a Museum telling the story of the town's lifeboat crews and boats. It houses the *Thomas Kirkwright*, Poole's first motorised lifeboat and famous as one of the armada of 'Little Ships' that helped take British troops off the beaches at Dunkirk in 1940. Poole's first lifeboat station was established in 1865 on the then deserted sand dunes at Sandbanks.

*Above*  A recent addition to events on the Quay is Bike Night, which takes place every Tuesday evening throughout the summer and has proved immensely popular, with both bikers and non-bikers alike. Over 1,000 bikers come to meet friends, compare bikes and enter the Bike of the Night competition. After the costs have been covered, surpluses are then donated to local good causes.

*Below*  The Quay at dusk.

*Above* Poole's historic hydraulic Lifting Bridge links Hamworthy to the town and allows yachts and shipping to enter Holes Bay. It was opened in 1927; its two halves each weigh 180 tonnes, but are so finely balanced they can be lifted by hand. Its timber Victorian predecessor had a hand-operated opening swing section in the centre, before which the only routes to Hamworthy were by ferry or a two-mile road journey. Plans are in place for a second lifting bridge known as the Twin Sails Bridge to be built across Holes Bay as part of a massive regeneration project.

*Right* A fishing boat passes the Sunseeker works on the Hamworthy side of the Quay. Sunseeker is one of Poole's greatest recent success stories. Originally known as Poole Powerboats, the company was founded in the 1960s by Robert Braithwaite, initially building a range of small powerboats. When the boat dealer and former Formula One driver Henry Taylor asked for one in white with a full width sun bed, Robert Braithwaite designed the Daycap 23, bridging the gap between sports boats and family cruisers. Since then a succession of new ever larger and more luxurious models have been built in the company's seven sites in Poole, virtually all of which are exported, establishing Sunseeker as a truly global brand. Today, the company makes between 250 and 300 motoryachts a year, employs 2,200 people and has a turnover of £240 million.

*Right* Fireworks light up the night sky. Throughout the summer, Poole plays host to weekly fireworks, street entertainments and live music.

Poole celebrates Harry Paye Day. Known as 'Arripay' to his French and Spanish victims, Harry Paye was a Poole sea-captain and privateer whose base was on Round Island and whose attacks on foreign shipping in the early 1400s gained him notoriety, wealth and the discreet approval of the king, Henry IV. One chronicle described him as 'a Knight who scours the seas'. His pillaging of the Spanish coast led to a revenge attack on Poole, in which prisoners were taken and the storehouses on the Quay set on fire. The photographs were taken on the 600th anniversary of Harry Paye's greatest triumph, an expedition of 1407 against the French during which he captured 120 coasting vessels laden with oil, iron and salt. He died in about 1419, and is buried in Kent.

HMS *Cattistock* combines Fishery Protection with countering the threat of mines, and is named after the village in west Dorset.

*Above* The statue of a lifeboatman outside the national headquarters of the Royal National Lifeboat Institution on West Quay Rd. Nearby is The Lifeboat College, which was opened by the Queen in 2004 for education and training. The Sea Survival Centre simulates the dangers and conditions regularly faced by lifeboat crews, from capsize drills in the wave pool, to engine room fires and a full mission bridge simulator where crews can experience live search and rescue situations at sea. In 2007, there were over 8,000 launches from the 233 lifeboat stations round the coasts of the United Kingdom and Ireland and 7,715 people were rescued.

*Above* Poole has two lifeboats of its own, a 3-man inshore rigid inflatable capable of 31 knots, and the *City of Sheffield,* seen here at its base near the Lifting Bridge. The 47ft Tyne Class lifeboat has been on station at Poole since 2001.

*Below* Trent Class lifeboat *Edward, Duke of Windsor,* alongside the Quay. The modern building in the background is Dolphin Quays, a block of 105 apartments occupying the site of the old Poole Pottery.

## Poole Today

*Above* The view west over the town centre and Harbour towards the Purbeck Hills from Seaview, Constitution Hill.

*Left* The ancient High Street has been the main route inland from the Quay since the town's medieval foundations.

*Below left* Today, the High Street ends in the open space of Falklands Square outside the Dolphin Shopping Centre. The Square owes its name to the part played in the Falklands War by the Royal Marines and Special Boat Squadron based at Poole. The Marines had first come to Poole in 1954 when they took over a wartime landing craft base and a combined operations base known as HMS *Turtle*. After returning from the Falklands, the Marines were awarded the Freedom of the Borough of Poole, and with it the right to march through the town, with bayonets fixed, drums beating and colours flying.

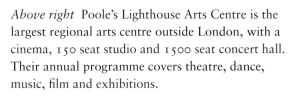

*Above right* Poole's Lighthouse Arts Centre is the largest regional arts centre outside London, with a cinema, 150 seat studio and 1500 seat concert hall. Their annual programme covers theatre, dance, music, film and exhibitions.

*Above* The Bournemouth Symphony Orchestra playing in its permanent home, the Lighthouse Arts Centre. Under a succession of recent conductors, the orchestra has established an international reputation, regularly recording and releasing CDs, touring abroad and playing to packed houses throughout the United Kingdom. It was founded by Sir Dan Godfrey in 1893 and has worked with many famous composers, including Elgar, Sibelius, Holst, Stravinsky, Vaughan Williams, Michael Tippett, John Tavener and Peter Maxwell-Davies.

*Right* The Civic Centre near the northern gates into Poole Park was opened in May 1932 and remains the administrative heart of the Borough of Poole.

A miniature railway, boating lake, drifts of flowers, even windsurfing or kayaking lessons – all are to be found in the 109 acres of Poole Park, which since its opening in 1890 by the Prince of Wales on land given to the town by Lord Wimborne, has been very much a people's park, enjoyed by all. There is also an indoor ice rink, a café, tennis courts, crazy golf, bowling green and an adventure playground for children known as Gus Gorilla's Jungle Playground.

# Poole Harbour

*Above* The smallest of the Harbour's five principal islands is Long Island, whose northern end is seen here from Arne. The channel between the two is a popular summer anchorage. Brownsea Island is in the background.

*Right* The beach at Shipstal Point, with not a footprint in sight. It's hard to believe that Shipstal Point is only the far side of the Harbour from a built-up conurbation of nearly 500,000 people stretching east as far as Christchurch.

*Following pages* An aerial view of Poole Harbour by Grahame Austin (Kitchenhams), with the cross-Channel ferry inward-bound between the Sandbanks peninsula and Brownsea Island. At its highest tides, the Harbour covers nearly 9,000 acres, making it one of the largest natural harbours in the world.

Sandbanks today includes some of the most expensive real estate in Britain, whilst the sheltered waters of the lagoon on Brownsea are home to a whole range of birds. In the centre to the left is South Haven Point and the chain ferry, with the Little Sea just visible. The islands to the left of Brownsea are Furzey Island and Green Island, whilst the Wareham Channel is visible in the far background, beyond Round Island and Long Island and Arne.

*Above* The high speed Condor car ferry *Condor Express* and the Brittany Ferries *Barfleur* alongside the Ferry Terminal at Hamworthy. The *Condor Express* goes to both the Channel Islands and St Malo, the *Barfleur* to Cherbourg. Commercial shipping in the Harbour is controlled by the Harbour Commissioners, who keep the channels dredged, provide pilots and make sure that the buoys and lights are maintained. Imports include timber, steel bars and girders, gas line pipes and palletised goods, whilst exports range from clay and grain, to sand and gravel and general cargo to the Channel islands.

*Below* The last of what was once a line of houseboats sits grounded by the tide in Bramble Bush Bay, with Brownsea Island in the distance.

*Above* Rockley Sands. Rockley Point is tucked away in the corner of the Harbour, and its quiet sheltered beach is easily overlooked in favour of the more popular beaches facing the open waters of the Channel.

*Right* Looking over Whitecliff Harbourside Park towards Parkstone Bay and the Parkstone Yacht Club marina from Whitecliff Viewpoint. The bird identification display in the foreground is a reminder of the wealth of the Harbour's bird life, which can total 20,000 in winter.

*Right* The Little Sea on Studland Heath, with the white chalk stacks of Old Harry on the right and Bournemouth on the left. The Little Sea is a quite recent addition to the Poole Harbour landscape, and was formed in Victorian times when two systems of sand dunes, one from the north, the other from the sea, finally met, turning part of Studland Bay into a freshwater lake. Today it is a haven for visiting wildfowl and freshwater birds.

*Below* Kite surfers add speed, colour and a rush of adrenalin to the shallow waters of Whitley Lake. When conditions are right, those less adventurous, or foolhardy, can watch them from Shore Road on the way out to Sandbanks.

*Right*   The distance sign on South Haven Point informs keen ramblers that Minehead is a 630-mile walk away along the South West Coast Footpath. South Haven Point marks the beginning of the footpath, which is the longest in Britain and includes Dorset's Jurassic Coast, Land's End and the wild North Cornish coast. There are celebratory markers at both ends, and this one by David Mayne incorporates a compass and pair of sails, together with wildlife and landmarks seen along the Footpath.

*Below*   Brownsea Island and the Harbour from Banks Road at sunset.

# Brownsea Island

*Above* Brownsea Island from Evening Hill.

*Below* Brownsea Castle and Quay. Hidden in the basement of the 18th century castle is part of the stonework of the original Tudor blockhouse, built by Henry VIII to defend the Harbour entrance. Brownsea's owners have included its share of eccentrics: one went mad, another committed suicide, a third bankrupted himself. The white building is the Family Pier, one of the extravagances of Colonel Waugh, whilst the battlemented line of cottages on the Quay was originally the Coastguard Station. In 1927 Brownsea Island was bought by the reclusive Mary Bonham-Christie, who forbade the killing of any animal on the island, including worms dug for bait, and refused to allow anyone to land on it. After the war, the 'Lady of the Lonely Isle' moved into one room in the Castle, in which she cooked, ate and slept. She died in 1961, aged 97, and her grandson gave the Island to the Treasury in lieu of death duties, who in turn handed it over to the National Trust, in whose care it happily still remains.

*Above* The stone commemorating the world's first Scout Camp on Brownsea Island in August 1907. The Scouting Movement was started by Robert Baden-Powell, a Boer War hero, who believed that living under canvas and learning self-reliance could help turn boys into men. The 22 boys of the first camp were woken by a blast on an African horn, followed by milk, biscuits and days spent stalking, tracking, building shelters and racing in boats. Today there are 16 million Scouts in 150 countries.

*Below right* The monks of Cerne Abbey built a chapel on the Island, but that was destroyed by the Vikings. A new church was finally built by Colonel Waugh in the 1850s, which stands amongst trees in the lee of the Castle.

*Above* Broken pottery litters the beach on Brownsea's west coast near Pottery Pier, all that now remains of a doomed attempt by a Victorian owner of the island, Colonel William Waugh, to start a semi-industrial pottery making terracotta bricks, stoneware pipes and cheap tiles. The Colonel built kilns, workshops, a tramway, a new pier, and a range of cottages for some of the 300 workers. Convinced that he was set to make a fortune he also restored the Castle, reclaimed 100 acres of marsh, and built the church. But his extravagance proved his undoing, and he was finally forced to flee to Spain, leaving debts of over half-a-million pounds.

*Above* Brownsea Island's most celebrated resident is the red squirrel, which thanks to living on an island and Brownsea's ample cover of Scots pine, whose cones provide food, has managed to avoid being driven out by the grey squirrel: this fine photograph is by Colin Varndell. There are also small colonies of red squirrels on Furzey and Green islands, which together with the Isle of Wight are now the only sites in which the red squirrel survives in southern England.

*Left* Brownsea Island, the South Shore. The chain ferry between Sandbanks and South Haven Point can be seen plying to and fro in the distance. This view of Brownsea beautifully captures its mix of woodland and scrub and sheltered shoreline.

# The Beaches

The beach at Sandbanks in high summer.

*Above* Looking west from near Canford Cliffs. Until well into Victorian times Poole's isolated beaches were most popular with smugglers, who found its shelving sand and easy access inland perfect for running their cargoes ashore. Today, all are recipients of Blue Flag awards. The water is clean, if chilly, and the swimming safe.

*Above* The gardens at the top of Canford Cliffs.

*Left* The beach huts at the foot of Canford Cliffs Chine. Poole Borough Council own approximately 1,200 beach huts in various locations, most of which are leased annually and for which there is a long waiting list.

*Above and right* The beaches at Sandbanks are the equal of any along the south coast. The view on the right is of the beach garden near the car park.

*Below* Shell Bay is only a short ferry ride away from the Sandbanks beaches, but its windswept dunes and empty beaches evoke a very different world. The long white building on North Haven Point is the Haven Hotel, which was built about 100 years ago. Few hotels can boast such a setting, and historically the Haven is important because it was where Marconi, the Italian pioneer of wireless, transmitted radio messages in the late 1890s. The chain ferry linking the two Points is the aptly-named *Bramble Bush Bay*, which entered service in 1994 and carries half-a-million cars a year between Sandbanks and Studland.

Out & About

*Above* The ruins of Corfe Castle can be seen from parts of the Harbour, but a morning spent strolling through the beautiful stone village followed by a climb up to the castle's ramparts is one of the delights of any visit to Dorset. The castle now belongs to the National Trust, and was built by William the Conqueror shortly after 1066. It was never a permanent royal residence, and the most famous episode in its history took place during the Civil War when it was held for the king by Lady Bankes, the wife of its owner. 'Brave Dame Mary' resisted two sieges before treachery allowed Parliamentary forces to enter the castle disguised as reinforcements. The castle was looted, its walls pulled down and its towers blown up, leaving the ruin that survives today.

*Below* Walkers enjoy the clifftop views from Handfast Point. 10,000 or so years ago, the chalk stacks of the Old Harry rocks were joined to the Isle of Wight at the Needles. The land linking them was finally breached by rising seas at the end of the last Ice Age. Even today, winter storms nibble away at the chalk. One stack, known as Old Harry's Wife, was washed away in 1896, leaving only a stump which is still visible at low tide.

*Above* The gardens at Compton Acres. The gardens were started in the 1920s, when Thomas Simpson, a margarine magnate, bought 10 acres in one of the many chines in Canford Cliffs. Today, the twelve linked gardens are one of Poole's most popular attractions, with glorious views out over the Harbour. Classical elegance and woodland walks combine with herbaceous borders, heathers, water gardens, and what is probably the best known of the gardens, the Japanese Garden, with its stepping stones, trees and tea house.

*Right* The paddle steamer *Waverley* in Swanage Bay. The 894 ton *Waverley* is the last sea-going paddle steamer afloat, and regularly cruises round Britain.

*Below right* Wealth from fish, extravagance, an imposter claiming to be heir to a fortune, a carpet-selling prince, gradual decay followed by a new lease of life – all are a part of the story of Upton House, seen here as it is today. The house was built in about 1816 by Christopher Spurrier, a Poole merchant, who bankrupted himself in the process. It next became embroiled in one of the most famous of English legal cases, that of the 'Tichborne Claimant', which was front page news in the 1870s, and concerned the failed attempt by a butcher's son who'd emigrated to Australia to claim that he was Sir Roger Tichborne and heir to the family estates, which included Upton. The next owners were the Llewellin family, who played a prominent role in Poole's affairs, and who in 1957 gave the house and 55 acres to the Borough. It was leased to Prince Carol of Romania who used it as a carpet showroom. In 1983, and thanks largely to the efforts of the Friends of Upton Park, the restoration of the house and gardens was finally started. Today the house is used for weddings and conferences, and forms the centrepiece of a Country Park Estate, open to all.

*Left* Poole's growth during the Middle Ages turned the once busy Saxon port of Wareham into a quiet backwater on the River Frome. Wareham is the gateway to the Purbecks, but is more attractive when approached by pleasure boat from Poole Quay. The journey takes you past the Cross-Channel Ferry Terminal, the landing craft and high-speed ribs on the slips of the Royal Navy Special Boat Service base at Hamworthy, before turning west and entering the winding reed-fringed River Frome, itself still lined with boats.

*Below* Early morning mist on the River Frome below Wareham.